MOTHER POEMS

Hope Anita Smith and her mother, Nedroe Lee Crews

MOTHER POEMS

words and pictures by
Hope Anita Smith

Christy Ottaviano Books
Henry Holt and Company
New York

Henry Holt and Company, LLC
Publishers since 1866
175 Fifth Avenue
New York, New York 10010
www.HenryHoltKids.com

Library of Congress Cataloging-in-Publication Data
Smith, Hope Anita.
Mother poems / words and pictures by Hope Anita Smith.—1st ed.
p.   cm.
"Christy Ottaviano Books."
ISBN-13: 978-0-8050-8231-9 / ISBN-10: 0-8050-8231-X
1. Mothers—Death—Poetry. I. Title.
PS3619.M587I57 2009   811'.6—dc22   2008018342

First Edition—2009 / Designed by April Ward
The artist used torn paper to create the illustrations for this book.
Printed in China on acid-free paper. ∞

10 9 8 7 6 5 4 3 2 1

For Lillian "Ma" Harrington,
whose heart was big enough
for one more—me. I love you.

—H. A. S.

Contents

MOTHER POEMS

Momma

I've got a momma
who combs and plaits my hair
with gentle soothing rhythms,
fingers dancing everywhere.

I've got a momma
who wraps me in her arms
like I'm some kind of present,
says I'm her lucky charm.

I've got a momma
who loves me through and through,
and can't nobody love me
like my momma do.

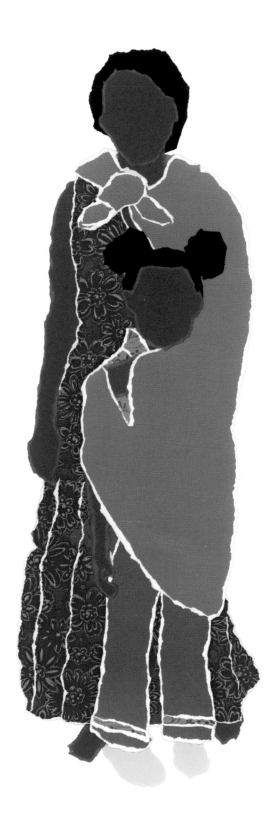

Superheroes

I know Batman has
a really cool car.
And Spider-Man can swing on a web
like Tarzan.
But I have a better superhero than that.
I know that Wonder Woman can
deflect bullets with her bracelets.
And the Bionic Man can leap thirty feet in the air
and has superhuman speed.
But I have a better superhero than that.
I have a superhero who lifts me out of
sorrow
and rocks me in her arms.
I have a superhero who knows how much
danger I'd be in without her
and travels the heart of darkness to come
back to me.
All other superheroes are just pretenders to
the throne
because I have the ultimate superhero,
the one with eyes in the back of her head.
She sees all and knows all.
She guards my closet door and keeps monsters
at bay.
She knits me a protective force field that
also keeps me warm at night.

She is always just where I need her to be.
Just when I need her to be.
She is the mother of all superheroes.
She is my mom.

Mothers Know

A mother knows
how to doctor.
When you're hurt
she patches you up with a Band-Aid.
Sometimes she can heal you with a kiss.
She is the best medicine.

A mother knows
how to fly.
When you are wobbly on your feet or
clumsy with a glass,
she is there
in a single bound,
donning her Supermom cape,
swooping you up in her arms,
averting disaster.

A mother knows
how to guide.
Helping you navigate
through hurt feelings and
bad choices.
Pointing you in the right direction
but letting you find your own way.
She is your North Star.

Mothers know.

In Her Shoes

I felt powerful.
Took on the world without
Fear or reservation.
I ka-lomphed around
in her shoes,
and each time they hit the floor,
the earth shook
(or at least the picture frames on the coffee table).
In her shoes
I was my mother.
Could do anything she could do,
and she could do
anything.
I steered clear of the things hanging in
her closet.
No clothes dragging me down or
tripping me up.
I wore her shoes,
and in her shoes—
my voice strong,
my smile big,
my heart happy—
I stood tall.

Sound Advice

"Get your hands off of your imagination,"
my grandma said to me.
And she and my momma laughed
long and loud
as they hugged me to them.
"You got to earn the right to
plant your arms akimbo.
You got to work a little harder.
You got to live a little longer.
You got to finish becoming a woman,
and then you can stand and
place your hands
upon your hips,
and your hips will hold them up."

Blues

Sometimes
things just don't go right.
Shoes won't lace,
zippers won't zip,
and buttons get all confused
and go through the wrong door,
making my shirts and sweaters
lean
even when I stand up straight.
My face wears a smile turned
upside down.
And I feel bad.
And I feel sad.
And I feel mad.

My momma wraps me in her arms
and says,
"Chile, you just got the blues.
Let me love 'em away."

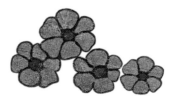

What My Mom Says

When I lose things,
my mom says,
"You'd lose your head if it wasn't attached to your neck."
When I ask,
"Why?"
my mom says,
"Because I said so!"
When I want to do something grown-up,
my mom says,
"You're too young."
When I try to get the last word,
my mom says,
"You're cruisin'!"
When I don't listen,
my mom says,
"It just goes in one ear and out the other."
When I ask for a bigger allowance,
my mom says,
"Money doesn't grow on trees."
But most of the time
my mom just says,
"I love you."

Imitation

Sometimes
I'm the mom
and I have six children.
Three dolls,
two fish,
and a dog.
And I get so tired because
I have to love them
all day long.
I have to squeeze them
and hug them
and kiss them.
And be proud of them
when they cry
or swim
or wag their tail.
And sometimes I have to
sit down for a minute
and catch my breath
'cause, Lord knows,
it's hard work
lovin' all these children.

Splinter

I remember playing on
the old wooden stairs at
Grandma's house.
They were good for
sliding down
on your bottom.
I would use my hands
to help propel me.
Much as I wanted to claim it,
it was not an original idea.
My mom told me how
she and her brother and sisters
had made it their life's work to rub each
step smooth.
My mom, Uncle Henry, Aunt Gladys, and the
twins, Earlene and Merlene—
they had all paved the way for me.
Every now and again,
some small piece of wood
would go against the grain
and find its way into the palm of my hand.
Momma would want to
pinch it out with tweezers
or use a needle to pick at it.
I was having none of that.

I held my hand close to my chest,
protecting it from her forms of torture,
and I cried crocodile tears as I waited
for Grandma to come with
her way of doctoring.
Grandma would get a wet crust of bread,
secure it over my wound with a bandage,
and let the water draw the splinter out.
It didn't take long and I never felt a thing.
When Grandma removed the bandage,
my palm would be new again.
She would rub the splinter into
the top of my head
for luck, maybe.
It always reminded me of the loaves
and the fishes in the Bible.
It's amazing what a grandma can do with
a little crust of bread.

Sleepover

Whenever my stepfather was
away on business,
I commandeered his side of the bed.
Lay claim to it by staking my bear
with one good eye and rubbed worn ears
on his pillow.
The nights I got to sleep with my mother
were a treat to be savored.
I didn't waste time arguing about bedtime,
pleading for another story,
or needing a drink of water.
It was time for sleep.
I would close my eyes
and grin from ear to ear
as I burrowed down into the covers.
I was having a sleepover
with my mother.
There was no greater joy.
But my mother
beside me
was never enough.
It wasn't long before the magnetic pull
of my love for her
had me curled up like a small stone
against her back.

Would that I were a stone that stayed put,
my mother often told me.
She had stories about how "the stone" gave
birth
to arms and legs and flung them
every which way.
One limb stopping to rest on her hip,
another on her head.
She said she would slowly inch herself away
from her many-tentacled child,
free herself from her minor entanglement.
But as soon as every connection
was broken,
an alarm sounded somewhere deep within me
and my foot would wander blindly,
yet purposefully,
across the cold sheet until it found
some part of her.
Once the connection was made,
the link in the chain restored,
my search was over and
I slept like a rock.
My mother said it always baffled her,
the way I could find my way to her,
even in sleep.

I could tell her, now,
if she were here.
She was
my touchstone.

While I Was Sleeping

When I knock on the neighbor's door,
it is dark out.
The world has gone to bed.
Miss Margie appears
all sleepy-eyed.
She's ready to be angry, but
she must see something in my face.
My mouth won't work, but my eyes are
screaming,
"Help me! Help my mother!"
Miss Margie races past me up to our apartment,
and I allow myself to be led into hers.
Her house is alive with activity now.
Everyone comforts me and tells me that
it's going to be all right.
I listen for sirens.
I count, "One thousand one, one thousand
two, . . ."
and then I hear them.
I allow myself to fall asleep
because help is here.
Everything *is* going to be all right.
So,
when Miss Margie wakes me up
and I see that she is wearing a sad little smile,

I know that she is thinking, "Poor thing.
What a scare you've had."
Out loud she says,
"Go with your father."
Her eyes are red.
As I march past her family
I know.
I know that everything is different now.
I know that I'm different now.
When we get home,
my father closes the door behind me,
throws his arms around me, and cries,
"Your mother didn't make it.
She's gone."
I find an air pocket and I breathe.
"It's okay to cry," he says. "Let it out."
But I don't cry.
I squeeze my eyes shut.
Try to make the tears flow.
But I don't cry because
I'm not sad that my mother is gone.
I'm just mad that she didn't take me with
her.

Duped

Everybody talks about
Death.
The thief who takes away people you love.
Kidnaps them.
Grabs them from their beds as they sleep.

Sometimes he waves wildly,
yells a big hello.
As if you know he's coming.
As if you sent him an invitation.

And sometimes he seems to
hurl himself through space and
(like Dorothy's house in *The Wizard of Oz*)
lands with a thud on some
unsuspecting someone.
And then they are gone.

But occasionally,
he sneaks up on you,
taps you on your right shoulder,
and when you turn to look,

he reaches over your left
and takes your mother.

It was the oldest trick in the book.
I can't believe I fell for it.

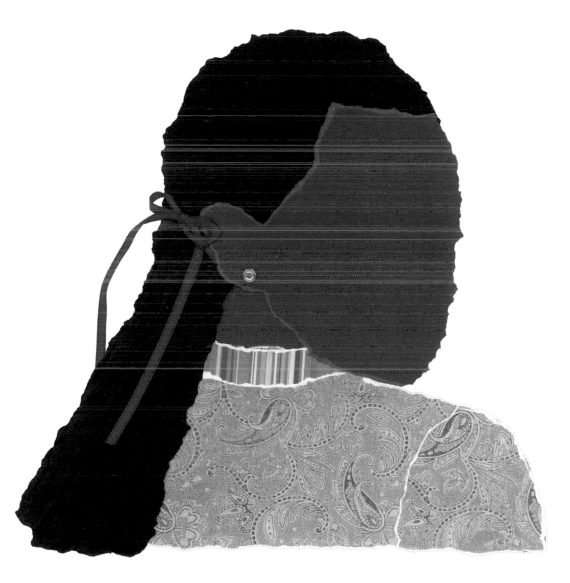

Conjugating Want

I WANT my mother,
so I took a picture of her
and slapped the word "WANTED"
in big block letters across it.
I made copies and posted them
in banks and post offices.
She wasn't *wanted* everywhere,
just here,
in my heart,
the place where her absence
had created an ache so deep
I had put up guard rails to keep myself from
falling in.
Yesterday, a man showed up
with a mother,
but she wasn't mine.
A case of mistaken identity.
He was so sure.

I don't know who was more disappointed.
His only reward was
to see me and my mother reunited,
and now
we are both wanting.

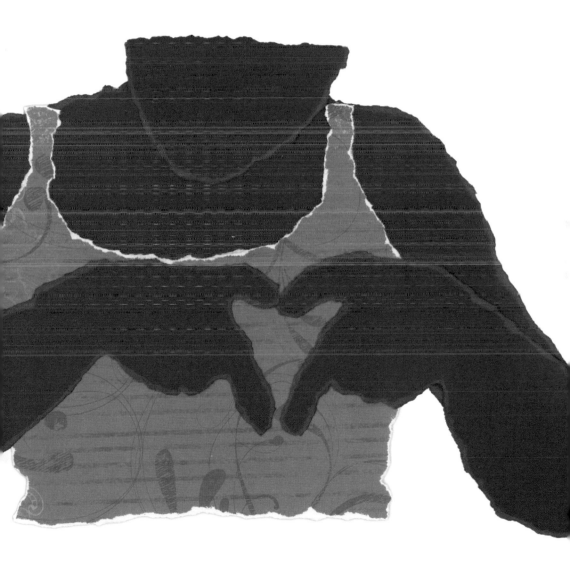

Let's Make a Deal

She's yelling at her mother.
Her words sound like those of an angry driver
who's leaning on the horn.
Her mother looks pale.
She can't speak.
She's trying to figure out what happened to
her daughter—
how she ended up with this
"other" child.
I stand off to the side,
and I'm thinking, Leave her.
Leave the little brat
right there.
Take me instead.
I would never talk that way to you.
You could hold my hand in the mall.
Even kiss me good night.
I'm not too big for kisses.
I close my eyes and pray.
Take me.
We both know
good daughters are hard to find.

Mother's Day

There were flowers.
An assortment of crepe- and tissue-paper flowers
with bright green pipe-cleaner stems
beautifully displayed
in a Fanta grape-soda bottle
papier-mâchéd in a rainbow of colors.

And there was a card
scrawled in an eight-year-old hand with a crayon
held so tightly you could see how hard each word was pressed
and where the colored wax pencil broke under that pressure.
HAPPY MOTHER'S (snap!) DAY!

There were tears
as I presented my gift to you,
strutting like a peacock, chest out, proud.
And then you hungrily swallowed me up in your arms.
I wanted to be devoured.
"Happy Mother's Day,"
my well-rehearsed line spoken right on cue,
slightly muffled by the walls of my prison.
I could hardly breathe.
I squirmed for air, but not too hard.
I wanted to stay locked up forever,
but then the warden came and unlocked the door.
I felt your arms fall away,

and I was pushed into the world with a
Ziploc baggie full of memories that
get heavier each time I pull
them out.

There were flowers.
A big white wreath wearing a
Miss America sash that said
"In Loving Memory."
No sweet aroma,
these are "worker" flowers
to say someone is dead.
Someone has passed on.

There were cards
covered in white lilies with ornate script that read
"Sorry for Your Loss" or
"Thinking of You During This Difficult Time."
When opened, they revealed a personal message
written by family and friends.

And there were tears.
So much sadness spilling out of me.
I cried as they presented me to you.
You were Snow White
waiting.
I should have kissed you,
but I was swallowed up by grief.

Someone's arms took me,
held me together.
But they are not your arms.
Besides, I know that they will let go.
"I want my mom!" I say it over and over
again,
but nobody hears.
My words are trapped inside me.
I let my chant lull me through life,
and when I awaken . . .
there are flowers.

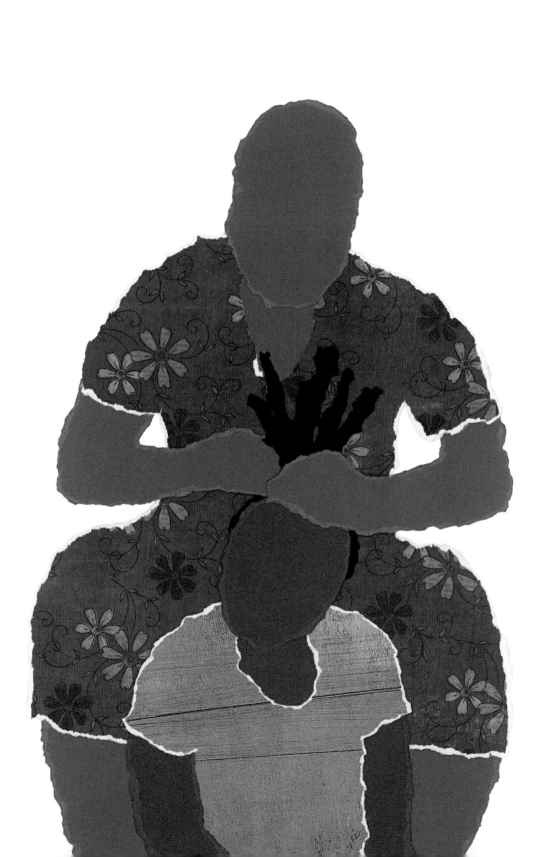

If I Had Said Good Night

I am twelve.
I am sitting between my mother's legs
as she does my hair.
My eyes are closed.
Our breathing is our only conversation,
but it is warm.
My mother's hands
weave my hair into braids,
but they also speak.
They announce, "You are safe."
They proclaim, "You are loved."
But then they stop their work.
I am startled out of my contentment.
"You finish up," she says.
My mother is tired.
I smile, and say,
"That's okay, Momma. You go to bed.
I can do it myself."
And then when she is gone in the morning—
gone in her sleep—
I am free to just
miss her.

Words

You never forget the last words. They stick with you
   night and day.
It doesn't matter if the words were kind or had a
   little bite.
You'll forever remember all the words you didn't say.

Words are a comfort, a sea of loving phrases. Jump in
   and play.
It's important. Get the inflection of what was said
   just right.
You never forget the last words. They stick with you
   night and day.

Time will eat away at them. They'll get old. They'll start
   to fray.
You hold on to them with both hands. Wrap each word
   and hold it tight.
'Cause you'll forever remember all the words you didn't say.

Outside, the weather says December; your heart says
   April, May.
Their words are always with you, walking around your
   heart in white.
You never forget the last words. They stick with you
   night and day.

Open up your mouth. Make sounds come out. You have
   to find a way.
So make a list. "I love you." "Sorry." And of course,
   "Good night."
You never forget the last words. They stick with you night
   and day.
And you'll forever remember the words you didn't say.

Good Behavior

I try to be good
(like when I was little).
I let someone else have
the bigger piece,
the seat by the window,
the first ride on my new bike.
I share
everything.
Give away toys,
books,
the doll with jet-black hair
and porcelain skin.
I am polite.
Say "please" and "thank you,"
"pardon me."
But it doesn't help.
My mother is still gone.
Tomorrow
I will try harder.

Rule #1

You don't learn it in school,
but it's true just the same:
You can't get mad at dead people.
You have to yell at your sister
or your dad or your best friend because
the person you're really mad at
isn't here.
Won't ever be here again.
I get mad just thinking about it.

My Mother's Kitchen

My aunt sings in the kitchen,
tries to woo food into tasting good.
She serves up "mystery meals" and waits
for us to pass judgment.
We all "Mmmmm" together
and raise our eyebrows ever so slightly,
hoping the gesture will act as a lever
to open our throats,
allow Aunt Nedra's
home cooking to pass through.

My mother could cook.
I could smell how much she loved me
every time she prepared a meal.
She shopped at the same market,
brought home the same ingredients,
but between the bag and the pot
something happened.
It was as if each item—potatoes,
tomatoes, green beans—
wanted to be *more* just to please her.
I wish I'd stood beside her in her kitchen,
my head resting against her hip,
committing her recipes to memory.
The "secret" ingredients.
The ones that couldn't be written down
because it wasn't about measurement.
But I only stayed long enough to
lick the spoon,
kiss the cook,
let my finger skate along the icing wall of
a cake.
My mother would smile or laugh,
squeeze me tight,
offer up a kitchen secret.
I was too busy for cooking instruction.

I breathed in the scent of my mother
mingled with the smells from her kitchen,
an intoxicating aroma.
I thought,
"Tomorrow. Tomorrow I will pay attention."
So many dishes are a disappointment to
me now.
Something is always missing.
Something I can't quite put my finger on.
Sad that secrets can't be passed on
from the grave,
and sadder, still, that I now know what it
is
to be hungry.

I love you more
eve in you. You'll u. You are special. I love yo
ou are spe do great things. You can do an I believe in you. Y d of you. You are beautiful. Yo
thing aby. I am so proud of you. You are ful. You are specin great things. You can do anyth
ua. You are goin l. always be n u. You are I
any always be my ba proud of yo ial. I love u are g so proud of you. Yo
can do anything. ou are special. I love u are goin ul. You ar going to do great thin
. You are beautifu ything. I believe i e in y can do anyth y baby. I am so prou
hings you. You are beautiful. yeautiful. You my ba you. You are bea You are going to
s to do great things. You e n lo an ou ca do anyth lie e in you. You anything. I bel
by. I am so u. I more. You a ll always b baby. I am so proud of I. You are beautiful. Y
gs. I beli ning. y more. You are g u'll are gs be my baby. I am so pi of you. You can do can
beautiful. Yo thing are beau you. You'll always be my ba ys be n you more ng to do great things. You are be
thing are beau you. You'll always be my ba ys be n you more s to do gre ing to do great things. Yo
great things. Yatiful. You are special u ba Yo more. Yo lly baby. I am so prou I am so proud of
You can do a ou can Y ou'll always You'll always more.

Give Me an "M"

When my mother died,
she was mourned by many.
The tooth fairy
hung up her wings,
went broke,
or became bored with my teeth.
(She still visited Corinne Baily, Yoshiko Bishop,
and Agatha Kramer,
but she never came to see me again.)
After the first disappointment,
waking to find my tooth
still there,
unclaimed, unwanted, unloved,
I stopped putting my small
white diamonds
under my pillow.
I had been duped.
My teeth held no real value
and so deserved no ceremony
and surely no reward.
It was my mother who had made me
believe
that I'd all but hung the moon
each time a tooth fell out of my mouth.
That's what mothers do.

Act as your personal cheerleader
when you are taking your first step,
tying your shoe,
losing a tooth.
Everything I did was amazing.
But now her pom-poms lie limp and
lifeless on the floor.
I claw at the ground, trying to
pick up the last remnants of her
confetti encouragement
so I can toss it into the air again—
paper applause,
dancing and twirling
in celebration of me.

Scabs

All my friends hate their mothers.
It's in the manual.
A rite of passage.
Because mothers
"think they know everything,"
"ask too many questions,"
"are soooo embarrassing!"
They even address them differently.
"Mo-ther," they say,
letting out a huff of air
as they roll their eyes,
bemoaning their horrible misfortune in getting
the *only* mother who knows *nothing*.
They march around together holding
invisible picket signs that say,
"Daughters Unite for Quality Moms" and
"We Want Another Mother NOW!"
I keep step with the daughters.
Try to look like I fit in.
But whenever I see mothers, I trip
myself up,
smile, hug them with my eyes.
Try to warm them with
the fire of love I felt for my mother
when she was still here.
It still burns within me.

The mothers smile back
with their eyes, and before I can blink,
they are gone
(you'd think they'd seen a ghost
daughter or something).
I go, too, sure that my betrayal is a
bad odor
that gives me away.
Their daughters have drawn a line in the sand,
and we have crossed it, the mothers
and I.
They, from one side; and me, from the
other,
and still we cannot meet in the
middle.

Cheated

I was cheated.
My mother never appeared to me in a dream.
Never stood across the room
in a heavenly glow,
saying nothing but letting her radiance
fill me up.
Never showed up and crocheted with me, our
favorite thing to do together,
one last time.
And I never woke, tangled in yarn, holding a
crochet hook tightly in my hand
(proof that it had really happened).
She never held my face in her hands,
looked me in the eye, and said,
"You're going to be just fine."
I could have used that assurance—
Ponette got it.
Her mother came to her
and told her she must learn to be happy
without her.
Countless others,
too many to name,
but not me.

When my mother left,
there was none of that
looking back.
I wish that she had been more like Lot's
wife.

Q and A

I never thought to ask my mother
what I was like when I was a baby.
Did I laugh a lot?
Was I fussy?
Did I have a favorite toy?
What was my first word?
When did I roll over? Crawl? Walk?
Did I ever like carrots?
Mothers give us our stories,
at least the beginning.
My mother left before she got a chance to
give me mine,
and I forgot to ask.
God should have made me smarter.
I am remembering less and less about my mother
and wanting to know more and more about me.

My Mother's Rule Book

What I remember most about
my mother
is her little rule book.
It was in the library of her head,
but it was a book just the same.
And I always knew
when she was telling me
something from that book because
she always spoke in
bold CAPITAL letters.
"HOLD MY HAND,"
whenever we were in a crowd.
It seemed like everyone wanted to be
where we were.
It was like we all had invitations
to the ball game or shopping mall
or carnival.
I would bring along
whatever stuffed animal or toy was
my companion at the time.
The day I lost one of them in the supermarket,
I had to question how much I loved it.
I had let it get away.
What if it were cold?
What if it were trapped somewhere
in the frozen foods?

If only I had listened to my mother when
she said,
"TAKE A SWEATER."
The toy and I would both be warm and safe
right now.
But I rarely brought a sweater
and forgot I had it with me even when I did
because it got in the way,
and my mother had long ago declared,
"I'M NOT CARRYING IT."
I would take my chances being cold,
catching my "death of cold."
I already believed that I was going to live
forever.
Sweaters and Sunday-school gloves
were just waiting for an opportunity
to get away from me.
I rejected them
before they had the chance to reject me.
There was usually some kind stranger who
would happen upon the lost article
and return it to me
by way of my mother.
And then they would both read aloud from
my mother's book
in unison:
"HANG ON TO IT."

I tried.
But I failed as often as I succeeded.
There was always something prettier, shinier,
to distract me.
I lost the mittens on a string.
I even lost the note
pinned to the inside of my jacket.
Because I knew that this losing
along with acne and broken hearts
would pass.
"YOU'LL GROW OUT OF IT,"
my mother assured me.
That's why my breath caught in my throat
when I overheard one woman say to another
in a hushed voice as she pointed to me,
"She lost her mother."
I thought,
"That's positively silly."
I loved my mother too much to lose her.
There was nothing prettier or shinier.
But what I wouldn't give to have some kind
stranger return her to me and admonish me
to "HANG ON TO HER, THIS TIME."
I would.
I am.
I am holding on to her as tight as I can.

Memory

I sometimes have thoughts of my mom that are
so concrete,
they bruise and batter me.
We are walking home, and she's
interrogating Donald Phillips,
only the cutest boy in the whole school.
Her X-ray vision can see the smile that
stretches across my face
even though she is walking behind us.
And then she takes that moment
to cash in on a lifetime debt that I owe
for taking twenty-three hours to be born.
"What are your intentions toward my daughter?"
she asks Donald
in front of everyone on the sidewalk
and people passing in their cars.

I can hear the roaring crescendo that is my voice:
"MOTHER!"
It is all so clear. Hard. Sharp.
I run toward it, forget to stop before I
hit it head-on.
It's a good memory because it is solid.
But there are others,
so many others
that are like clouds floating by.
I stop what I am doing, lie down on a patch
of grass to enjoy.
We are doing—something; and I am—happy? sad?
angry?

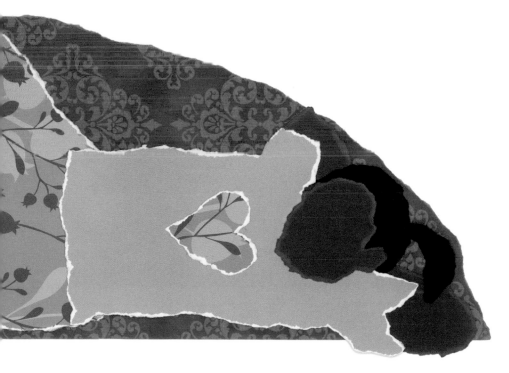

And my mother—
laughs with me? Comforts me? Sends me to my
room?
"Be still," I tell the sky.
I just need to look at the cloud a moment longer.
I almost have it—
but it's gone.
It has drifted off to blend
and change shape
with a thousand other memories.
The dark clouds roll in,
and the ache in my heart
rumbles like thunder.
And there is a lightning flash of my
mother
so bright I have to look away.
I count,
"One thousand one . . .
one thousand eight, . . ."
because it lets me know how far away the
memory of her is.
And then the sky opens up and rains.
I rain, too.

Dangerous Game

I saw her when I went out one day.
She asked me if I wanted to play.
I should have turned the other way.
This is a dangerous game.

"Come be a part of my family.
We'll add you to the family tree."
Someone else's mom and she wants me.
This is a dangerous game.

She didn't have to explain the rules.
I ranked #1 in "daughter school."
Having a mom again would be so cool.
This is a dangerous game.

I play my part just like a pro.
I can't believe how much I know.
My head says stay, my heart says go.
This is a dangerous game.

It seems that I'm always wanting more.
I've become quite good at keeping score.
If I were her I'd show me the door.
This is a dangerous game.

I learned the game and I play it well.
But I'm always scared, and there's no one
to tell.
I should have stayed in my
motherless shell.
This is a dangerous game.

Sleuthing

Some things are hard to find—
elementary, my dear.
Especially when you're not exactly sure
what you're looking for.
But I am taking this case.
I don my Sherlock Holmes cape and hat
and begin searching for clues,
looking for answers.
The new mother keeps saying
she loves me.
I don't touch a word until I put on gloves.
I don't want to taint the evidence.
I drop each word into a plastic bag,
label it "Exhibit A."
There are hugs strewn about,
kisses splattered all over
the walls of my heart.
Everything is out of whack.
My head is reeling.
I must have been hit from behind,
but there was no forced entry.
All the windows are closed
except the one in the steam room,
the place where I rage about MY mother
being taken away from me.
It can get really hot in here.

I could burst into flames without a breeze
coming in now and again.
The neighbors are milling about outside,
craning their necks to catch a glimpse
of what's going on.
I feel their eyes on me,
but the new mother
is undaunted by the crowd,
uses her coat to cover me
as we walk to the car.
Down at the station,
I ask questions
and just when I think there is no way
I can get a confession,
she opens her heart wide,
takes me in
her arms like a bellows fanning away
all my inquiry,
my doubting,
my hours of interrogation.
With her arms wrapped around me
her eyes say it all—
Stop searching for evidence to convict me.
I did it.
I love you.
And if given the opportunity
I'd do it again.

Mother Lovin'

I imagine
her arms wrapped around me,
and I remember the warm feeling I'd get
when she'd nuzzle her face into my neck.
She said she was sniffing out the baby in me.
I didn't know what she meant.
At eleven, I was years away from being a baby.
Surely, that scent,
the one only a mother can know,
was long gone.

My mom used to tell me the story of
when I was born.
How she was so happy when they handed
me to her
that she could barely see me through her
tears,
but her hands touched every inch of me,
making an outline that her arms conformed to.
And then she lifted me up to her chest,
burrowed her nose in my neck
and breathed me in.
She said that when she smelled my baby scent
her happiness was complete.
She knew that I was her baby.
I loved that story.
And even though I pretended to be annoyed by
her motherly affections,
I never felt more loved than when she
wrapped me in her arms.
I remember
her nose is nestled in my neck,
she breathes in,
drawing my baby smell to the surface,
and I know
she has found it when
she holds me tighter

and rattles off a round of
machine-gun kisses.
"I remember," she would say.
"And when I hold you,
I am there."
And I am there, too,
remembering the kid I used to be,
being scooped up into my mother's arms
for some Mother Lovin'.

Instructions on How to Lose a Mother

Someone will tell you that your mother is
gone.
They will say it quietly, but to you, it will be
loud and shrill.
The sound will shatter you.
You must pick up all the pieces
and put them away for safekeeping.
Do not attempt to put yourself back
together.
It is too soon.
You will only wind up cutting yourself.
This is a puzzle that no longer has a map.
You don't know what it's supposed to look like.
You wouldn't know where to begin.
Here's the hard part—
wait.
Every time you think you're ready,
wait.
Instead,
look through old photo albums and memories.
See yourself with your mother.
Whole. Complete.
Weep for that self.
She is gone. Dead, too.

And then you must wade through your tears,
being careful not to let waves of anger and
fear
pull you under and hold you there.
When you make it to higher ground,
wring yourself out,
lay your head on a cozy bed
or in the lap of someone who cares about you,
and sleep.
Because now it is time to begin
the impossible task of putting you back together,
one piece at a time.
Be careful.
There is a good chance you will still cut yourself
(that risk isn't gone just because you followed directions).
But if a sharp edge slices through,
it is because you are finally committed to
the new you.
You have stopped looking back.
When you have fitted all the pieces together,
hold it up,
marvel at your new reflection.

Constructing Trees

I could feel it coming.
Like wild horses galloping toward water,
I could feel Christmas coming to me.
My mom and I would bring it
up from the basement.
Ornaments, holiday decorations, and
our tree,
lying dead in its coffin,
its epitaph on the lid.
No "R.I.P." here;
instead
"A.R.,"
"Assembly Required."
We grew our tree,
my mother and I,
from the base to the tree topper.
We raised the tall pole, and I held it
with two hands
while my mother wrestled
the green-tipped branches
into the green ring around the base,
and then we worked our way up,
matching the color tips to the ring colors
around the pole:
red, yellow, blue, black, brown, orange, white,

and another color that had long since
disappeared.
If we counted the rings,
our tree was nine years old.
It took some time, making a tree.
Every year, it got a little harder.
The colors became fainter.
But we didn't care.
I marveled that we were doing a thing
only God could do.
We were making a tree.
We dressed it in colored lights, ornaments,
and silver strands of tinsel.
When we were through,
we would stand back and admire it.
And right before our eyes,
like Geppetto's Pinocchio,
it became real.

I build trees all the time now.
Memory trees.
I start at the base,
my earliest memory,
and work my way up.
Hang moments with my mom in my mind.
Some of them real, some imagined.
All of them shining.